Change Your Career

10 Practical Steps to a Successful Career Change

Adora Ikwuemesi

maxhouse
MEDIA

Copyright © 2018 by Adora Ikwuemesi

The right of Adora Ikwuemesi to be identified as the author of this work has been asserted by her.

All rights reserved. No part of this book may be reproduced, stored in a retrieval system, or transmitted, in any form, or by any means (electronic, mechanical, photocopying, recording or otherwise) without the prior written permission of the author, except in cases of brief quotations embodied in reviews or articles. It may not be edited amended, lent, resold, hired out, distributed or otherwise circulated without the publisher's written permission.

For any enquiries regarding this book, please email:
publisher@maxhousemedia.com

Although the author and publisher have made every effort to ensure that the information in this book was correct at press time, the author and publisher do not assume and hereby disclaim any liability to any party for any loss, damage, or disruption caused by errors or omissions, whether such errors or omissions result from negligence, accident, or any other cause.

First edition

ISBN: 978-1-9165037-0-0

Published by Maxhouse Media

Cover design by Adam Renvoize
Interior formatting by Mark Thomas / Coverness.com

Change Your Career

This book is dedicated to Michael, Zinachukwudi and Chukwuzita.

Table of Contents

Acknowledgements i

Introduction iii

How to Use this Book v

1. Start with a Vision 1

2. Retrain 7

3. Highlight Transferable Skills 15

4. Gain Experience 25

5. Consider Internal Vacancies 33

6. Consider the Industry 39

7. Consider Easier Entry Points 47

8. Get Better at Networking 53

9. Plan Your Finances 61

10. Set Goals and Execute 69

11. Bonus Tip: Be Patient 75

About the Author 79

"There is no passion to be found in playing small, in settling for a life that is less than you are capable of living."

–Nelson Mandela

Acknowledgements

I would like to thank everyone who helped with this book or supported its development in any way. A special thank you goes to my father for reading the initial article and suggesting that it would make a great book.

Introduction

If you are reading this book then you have made a decision to change a very important aspect of your life. It is not unusual to change your career several times throughout your work life. According to career change statistics, the average person will change careers five to seven times during their working life. In fact, a career change is inevitable for most people.

A question I often get asked by people who want a career change is how: 'How can I make the transition to a new career in the quickest and smoothest possible way?' A key concern for those starting their careers is how they can forge ahead in the job market, while more experienced workers are more concerned with how to make a transition that takes into account their previous experience while minimising financial loss. Despite concerns, a career change is possible at any age and at any stage in life. When you know how to change your career, the process becomes easier and quicker.

Change Your Career is a practical guide to achieving your career aspirations. Whether you are starting your career, changing your career or starting a business, this book will help you. Each chapter will guide you through practical actions that you can take to get to your desired career destination faster.

I have personally made five career changes in my lifetime, two within related fields and three to unrelated fields. My career profile mirrors a zigzag spanning the fields of information technology, telecoms, management consultancy, human resources management and entrepreneurship. I did it five times and each time for a different reason: sometimes to fulfil dreams, other times to adapt to changing priorities. Whatever your reason, you deserve the change you desire. You are almost there and I am wishing you the very best!

How to Use this Book

This book comprises eleven chapters. The first ten chapters represent ten actions you can take towards achieving a successful career change. The last chapter concludes with a bonus tip. Each chapter ends with a task that you are required to complete. As each task requires some writing, you may need a notebook and pen or a device that allows you to take notes.

I suggest you work with a notebook where you can complete the tasks outlined in each chapter. It is advisable that you use the same notebook for all the tasks so that you can easily reference it in future. It is also exciting to come back to the notebook in a few months or even years and appreciate the progress you have made.

If you choose not to write or do not have immediate access to a notebook, you can reflect on the questions and tasks in each chapter and plan to write them down later.

The reason why I advise you to write in a notebook is because writing is a great way of clarifying and articulating your thoughts and plans. Many people attest to writing being therapeutic as well as playing a big part in the planning and action-taking required for achieving set goals.

Regardless of your preferences, this book is an easy read and will help you achieve a successful career change.

Change Your Career

1

Start with a Vision

If you don't know where you are going, you will end up everywhere and nowhere.

A vision is a mental picture of a future destination. A career vision depicts the dream you have for your career, who you want to be and where you see yourself in the future. With increasing lifespans, a person's career can last 60 years. It may help you to know that whatever you are experiencing now in your career is only a small part of the long career life you are going to have. Creating a vision, knowing that you may still have a long way to go, can help steer your efforts in the right direction.

Having no vision for your career is like sailing a ship without a destination in mind. Without a clear destination, the ship will sail with the tides and end up wherever the wind takes it. Without a vision, it is very easy to get distracted because you do not have a clear idea of where you are going. If you come across a new career option, you will probably join the bandwagon since you have no firm grip on a particular career path. This lack of clarity will keep swaying you in different directions.

I have had my fair share of visionless career journeys. I probably had more vision as a child than I did during early adulthood. As a child, I remember wanting to write books, and then, at another point, I wanted to be a journalist. Both of these careers are somewhat similar to what I am doing now, as I am, indeed, writing a book. As I grew older, especially as a teenager, I was beyond confused. Between peer pressure and wanting to please my parents, it seemed like my career choices changed daily. Everyone thought I would become a lawyer because I was articulate from a young age. I also considered accounting, but then I realised I hated numbers. As I could not make up my mind, I settled for studying for an Economics degree as I was good at Economics during my A-levels. Despite choosing a course I had earlier enjoyed, I somehow ended up not enjoying it at university-level. I really wish my zigzag career journey had ended right there, but it did not, and I ended up making several other career changes before I started heading in some sort of direction.

After the unfulfilling experience I had studying Economics at university, I attempted to craft a vision for my future career. Remembering my childhood desire to become a writer, I considered studying Communications for my Master's degree.

But at 21 years of age and with no clear direction, it didn't take much for me to get swayed in an entirely different direction again. When I heard from a friend that Information Technology jobs paid higher and were much sought-after, I changed my planned course of study from Communications to Information Technology without even batting an eyelid. Without a vision, you end up everywhere and nowhere.

Now a career vision is nothing complicated. All it encapsulates is deciding what you want for your career life. Like every part of life where we dream of our future, our career vision simply articulates our career dreams. Some people, for fear of not being able to achieve their dreams, are scared to even articulate them. The simple truth is that visions do not have to be realistic. Visions are futuristic; you do not need to have the resources required to get somewhere in order to dream of going there. You just need to imagine it to dream it.

Many creations we enjoy today happened because individuals dared to dream. These people envisioned what had seemed to be impossible things at that point in time. Walt Disney, the founder of Disneyland, had a vision to build a theme park where both parents and their children could have fun. Today, Disneyland is known as the happiest place on earth, where dreams and happiness are said to meet.

If it is not yet clear to you what you want for your career, it may be clear to you what you don't want. At least that is how it worked for Oprah Winfrey, the media mogul. She wasn't very sure who she wanted to be but was very sure she did not want to live a life like her grandmother had – hanging washed clothes on the line. Knowing what you want and what you don't want are two sides of the same coin. Knowing what you don't want can help you articulate what you do want. Knowing you do not want to work in an office may help you realise that you want to work in the field or independently or even from home.

Vision boards are another way to articulate your dreams, although they are often used to represent areas of life beyond your career. A vision board is a visual tool that can help you define and focus on a specific life goal. There are many people, including celebrities such as Ellen DeGeneres, who attribute their success to creating vision boards. There are no hard and fast rules on how a vision board should look, but often they are boards that display pictures, cut-outs or words depicting a desired future. The important thing is to create something that articulates and focuses on where you want to be and is designed in a way that resonates with you.

The story of Jim Carrey, the Hollywood actor known for his unique comedy style, is often portrayed as a creative example for envisioning your future. We are told that, years ago, as a struggling comedian, he was booed off the stage at a comedy club. Rather than feeling discouraged, this experience served as a turning point for him. Carrey is said to have pushed on to pursue his passion, and, in a unique way, he visualised his own success by writing himself a cheque for $10 million, adding a note that read 'for acting services rendered'. Today, it is obvious to all that his dreams came true. A few years ago, while using the bathroom in a CEO's office, I saw a cheque for a large amount of money. It was written in the name of the CEO and pasted on the bathroom mirror. When I asked the CEO what it was for, he told me that it was his desire to be paid that amount by a client some day and, so, he was envisioning it.

A vision is simply future casting. It is about creating the type of future we desire. Whatever style of visioning works for you, do it – the important thing is to dream it.

Still not sure what your career vision is? Try completing the following task to help clarify your thoughts and put together a more vivid description of the desired future for your career.

Task 1

1. Write a story that describes your ideal career. Imagine yourself in the future and as having achieved the highest level of career success. What will you have accomplished? What does your life look like? What kind of work will you do? Who will you work for? Where will you be? What kind of hours will you work? Who will you work with? Write down as much as you can on how a successful career looks to you.

2. In just one paragraph, write your career vision and a description of how you plan to achieve it.

2

Retrain

One of the obvious gaps for anyone who wishes to change careers is a skills gap.

A skills gap refers to the difference between the skills requirements of a job role and the current level of skill you possess. Right now, you may be reading this book because you do not have the adequate level of know-how or the skill set to perform your dream role optimally. To become more suitable for a role, you have to minimise the difference between the required job skills and the skills you possess. Skills gaps need to be closed, and, if you want to be taken seriously by potential recruiters or employers, you need to demonstrate what you have done to close your knowledge and skills gap.

One of the surest ways to demonstrate your desire for a career change is via investments into improving your knowledge and skills. Investments such as spending time and money developing your knowledge and skills indicate focus and determination. Any individual who does not take personal responsibility of his or her personal development is only limiting his or her opportunity for growth in a fast-changing world.

Retraining is a must-do endeavour if you want to keep advancing in any career. Retraining options can take different forms, so it is important to consider your options carefully and pick the option most suitable for you at any given time. For example, there may be options such as postgraduate programmes, short courses, professional certifications, on-the-job training or apprenticeship in your desired field. Ensure that you identify which option fits well into your growth needs and then be ready to go for it. Sometimes what you need could be a combination of two or three of these training options.

I have personally retrained several times in my career in order to fulfil varying career goals and keep my skills relevant. I started out with my first degree, which was in Economics, and then I took my Master's degree in Information Technology, after which I embarked on a Diploma in Psychology, in addition to becoming a certified HR professional. More recently, I completed a professional coaching course. Doing all of these was not easy, as it took me time, money, energy and a good dose of commitment. However, that was the price I had to pay to support my career changes and growth. Every single training programme I invested in was because of a change in my career path. I chose a Master's degree in Information Technology because I wanted to get a higher paying job, and, at the time, careers in Information Technology were highly sought-after. Yet again, after about five years in the Information Technology field, I found myself developing more interest in a career that was people-oriented, so I immediately enrolled for a Diploma in Psychology. It was an intensive one-month programme, but I used up all of my annual vacation to ensure that I achieved it alongside my full-time job.

Career advancement requires investment and does not come easily. If you want a career change, be prepared to invest your money and time. I strongly believe Benjamin Franklin, who said that 'an investment in knowledge pays the best interest'. An investment in your career development is money well spent as it is an investment in your future. What better investment can there be than the one that prepares you to create or take advantage of varying opportunities for successes that lie ahead? Investing in yourself is the foundation of all your future investments. You cannot give what you do not have.

While organisations are charged with the responsibility of providing the work environment, tools and culture that support the growth of their staff, it is wise to avoid limiting your personal development to the training budget of your organisation. A mistake some employees make is to totally rely on their employers for their personal development. You don't have to rely on your employer; you can take charge of your career today by being proactive. Plan ahead and be forward-thinking and future-ready.

Having a stable, well-paid job or being experienced in your current career is no reason to throw your hands in the air and do away with updating your skills. The world is changing rapidly, organisations and markets are being disrupted, and robots are taking over jobs. To stay relevant in the job market, continuous development is inevitable. Be intentional about growing your skill set, pushing yourself beyond your comfort zone and committing to learning new things and new ways of doing things.

The same principle applies to employees considering becoming business owners or entrepreneurs. You can save a lot of time and energy if you gain adequate knowledge of and skills around your intended endeavour. People who want to start a business in an area in which they have little or no experience should keep in mind that one of the surest ways to minimise the risk of failure is to gain a good understanding of the business you wish to begin. I have worked with several business owners who started their businesses in this way. In particular, one started a restaurant business; part of his career plan was to develop a solid understanding of the restaurant industry. To realise this, he went on to pursue an MBA focusing on Restaurant Management. He did not want to take any chances, so he wanted to get as much knowledge as he could to improve his chances of business success. Today, he runs a successful chain of restaurants. Sure, there are no guarantees even with all the knowledge in the world, but knowledge, they say, is power, and it sure puts you at an advantage.

It may appear as though all the training I am referring to is academic or formal; however, a lot of training can be informal and self-directed too. After all, not everyone has the funding to pursue higher degrees or professional certifications. Indeed, all of us also have individual differences when it comes to learning styles. Some people are visual learners, while some learn better by listening and some by practising.

In this information age, learning independently is ever-so prevalent and much easier than it was, as the internet provides us with reams of information in a few clicks. Learning has never been more accessible. There are thousands of online courses and YouTube videos that anyone with internet access can view and learn from.

With all this, it is now possible for people to train themselves without leaving the comfort of their homes. Using your smartphone, you can read articles, watch training videos and even complete the highest forms of qualifications in a lot of fields. There has never been a better time to learn everything you need to know.

If you are someone whose learning style can be fulfilled via the opportunities provided by technology, then your only requirement is the discipline to follow through to the end. Motivation doesn't always come easy, so you may need to remind yourself of the benefits you will gain by staying on track.

So, whether you are changing jobs or starting a new business, determining and then embarking on the right type of training is a crucial activity that greatly improves your likelihood of success.

Answering the following questions will help you identify what knowledge and skills you need to gain for your dream career or job, where you are now and what you need to do to close your knowledge and skills gap. Remember that all results stem from actions, so it is important that action is taken to see the change we desire in our career.

Task 2

1. What knowledge and skills are required by your desired career?

2. What knowledge and skills needed by your desired career do you currently possess?

3. What is the gap between the required skills (1) and your current skills (2)?

4. What are your training and development options (for example, short courses, postgraduate course, online learning, professional exams)?

5. Which of the training and development options will you take?

6. In what time frame will I begin and complete this training?

3

Highlight Transferable Skills

Transferable skills are those skills that you have acquired that can be transferred to other careers as well.

They can be developed in one situation and used in another, hence the name transferable skills. They are skills developed through personal experience in areas such as school, sports, work and life in general. They are sometimes called soft, generic or people skills. Though often overlooked, they are incredibly valuable as they can be applied to a variety of jobs and industries. Examples typically fall under the broad categories of interpersonal, communication, leadership and organisational skills. Whether you are new to the job market or a highly experienced executive, the good thing is that everyone has transferable skills.

Because transferable skills cut across several careers, they can be particularly useful when you have little or no work experience in a particular field. Having transferable skills demonstrates that you already have some of the required competencies for the new career or job you are targeting. For example, customer service skills are critical for any role that requires managing people or clients. The fact that you have managed relationships with clients is a good precedent for roles in human resources or sales, which require good interpersonal and customer-focused skills. Never underestimate the importance of transferable skills, as they can be the one factor that gives you that edge. Some people do themselves an injustice by ignoring their transferable skills when preparing for a career change. The good news is that you can avoid that mistake by ensuring that you leverage your transferable skills from today.

Gaining transferable skills is a critical reason why individuals should take the initiative to learn beyond their current role, as all learning is an opportunity to acquire new knowledge and skills that could prove useful in other roles. Opening yourself to new learning opens you up to acquiring new competencies, and that exposure is often crucial for other roles. Sometimes, these competencies may appear irrelevant to your current career, but, eventually, they turn out to be helpful in another career you may choose to pursue later on in life. A phrase I keep close to my heart is 'no knowledge is lost', and this is because I have experienced several circumstances where I finally got to use knowledge or experience that I had thought, at the time, was a waste of time.

I remember learning certain concepts in high school and as an undergraduate. I remember thinking then that it was all theory and that I would never use most of the knowledge. Today, it has become a different ball game. Just the other day, I mentioned the phrase 'action and reaction are equal and opposite'. I recently realised it was Newton's third law of motion, which states that 'for every action, there is an equal and opposite reaction'. For someone who was terrible at Physics, I was not sure where that knowledge came from. I also thought the term 'opportunity cost' was just an Economics textbook concept. However, in more recent times, more than 25 years after learning that concept in high school, I find myself constantly referring to the opportunity cost of continuing with certain decisions. My point is that you never know when certain knowledge that appeared irrelevant will become relevant.

Never downplay your transferable skills; they could be your lifeline to your new role or promotion. What you may consider an unimportant skill may just be what will make you stand out in that next career path you desire. Use every opportunity before you to learn new skills and refine your old ones. People who are able to demonstrate the relevance of their transferable skills to a potential employer stand a better chance than those who cannot. Similarly, the better you can demonstrate the relevance of your current skills to your new role, the better your negotiation power at the interview table.

I have personally benefitted from relying on my transferable skills during all my career changes. I was able to demonstrate that the skills I acquired from previous jobs were very relevant to the job I was applying for and, as such, was able to avoid pay cuts.

My first job role after graduating with a Master's degree in Information Technology was as part of an IT helpdesk team, providing IT support to over 6,000 users of a charity organisation. When I became dissatisfied with the role, I applied for a role as a Design Engineer for Nokia UK, a telecoms firm. I studied the job description in detail, and it was apparent that the role mainly involved writing technical documents for programmers. I had acquired some technical writing skills during my postgraduate degree project. My project involved designing an online help system for a software application. I had also been involved in updating my IT helpdesk team's support manual, which gave step-by-step instructions on resolving user problems.

During my interview with Nokia, I was able to demonstrate the relevance of my existing skills to the advertised role. I did not have a technical background aside from my Master's degree, but the conversation was focused on my transferable skills and their relevance to the new job. The required qualification for the job was a Bachelor's degree and the required experience was one to two years. After a successful interview, I was offered the base salary. On receipt of the offer, I rejected the initial offer and asked for an upward review. Despite having only nine months' work experience, I was able to negotiate a higher salary by demonstrating that my skills exceeded the base rate salary due to my postgraduate degree and transferable skills. My request was accepted and I was given a revised offer letter.

Throughout my career, my competence in writing has helped me in all of my major career changes. Who would have thought that writing was such a versatile skill? I have always liked to write, and, all through my career, I have continued to seek opportunities to write; this one transferable skill has led me to have more fulfilling careers.

Even while studying information systems, when I was given the opportunity of choosing my project from a list of options, I chose to develop the online help system because the bulk of the project involved writing the help manual before converting it to an online application. It was this same experience that became the leverage in my second career change, when I moved from IT to telecoms. Despite bearing the title of Design Engineer, the key skill involved in the telecoms role was writing technical specifications and documentation for programmers. When I made my next career change, to consultancy, I applied the same experience gained from writing to developing training materials and writing client proposals and reports. Today, I am writing this book, which gives me leverage for a career as an author.

Sometimes, even when the journey is not as straightforward, just follow the dream and follow the skills that you enjoy using. As you build your skills, you begin to have a clear advantage; that clear advantage is leverage, and leverage is a winning strategy.

Today, after having gained the opportunity to hire for clients and my own organisation, I have hired people for their transferable skills, even when their technical skills were not that impressive. Technical skills are great, but, wherever they are difficult to find, you will find employers hiring people who already have transferable skills, with a plan to train them in technical skills. I often look out for transferable skills such as communication and problem-solving skills in all roles and leadership skills in more senior roles. Even people with little experience can demonstrate leadership skills by indicating examples of when they have been responsible for leading and managing a team of people. You may have experience in a leadership role in your community, your church or even in your household; one needs to remember that all these experiences count. The same applies if you are interested in starting a new business. There are a lot of relevant skills you already possess due to your previous roles, and, regardless of what you were doing, some of these will definitely count and prove useful in your new venture.

While you are focused on the future and planning a career change, learn to take stock of all your skills and highlight the ones that are transferable to your new career. Take time to further develop these skills and, when the opportunity comes for you to make a career move, project them to your potential employer or use them to your advantage in your new business.

The next task will help you identify your transferable skills. Provided below is a list of transferable skills. The list is nowhere near exhaustive, but it is a good start and one you can definitely expand on. Once identified, it will be useful to keep a mental note of them, especially as they relate to any future role you may be interested in.

List of Transferable Skills

Communication
Speaking effectively
Writing concisely
Listening
Giving feedback
Expressing ideas
Expressing feelings
Negotiating
Persuading
Developing rapport
Facilitating discussions

Leadership and management
Managing teams
Delegating responsibilities
Planning
Coordinating tasks
Solving problems
Managing conflict
Making decisions
Taking action
Motivating others
Coaching others

Planning and research
- Identifying requirements
- Setting goals
- Planning action
- Monitoring projects
- Gathering data
- Evaluating results
- Analysing data
- Interpreting data
- Reporting data
- Disseminating information

Self-management
- Managing time
- Managing stress
- Prioritising tasks
- Meeting deadlines
- Working well under pressure
- Self-awareness
- Self-control
- Self-confidence
- Self-motivation
- Self-preservation

Teamwork and interpersonal
- Sharing success
- Accepting responsibility
- Contributing to team effort
- Encouraging others' ideas
- Developing rapport
- Respecting others' opinions
- Negotiating
- Persuading others
- Influencing others
- Getting along with others

Task 3

1. List as many transferable skills as you can think of that you possess. You can review some of those included in the list provided.

2. Write down at least five other things that you believe you enjoy or are good at doing.

3. Write down at least five things that people say you are good at doing. Learning new things; reading people; anticipating issues; thinking on my feet; disseminating info (explaining)

4. Using up to ten of these transferable skills, try writing complete sentences describing how you use these transferable skills (for example, I am good at writing reports; I am good at persuading people to see my perspective)

4

Gain Experience

From my many years of working as a human resources consultant, one of the things I know for certain is that although academic qualifications are often a criteria in most professions, employers place significant value on work experience. In some professions, getting certified is simply endorsed evidence of work experience and not replacing the work experience itself. From an employer's perspective, having experience can indicate two important factors worth considering: the reduced costs of training and the increased probability of the employee hitting the ground running. These two factors are important to most employers, especially in smaller businesses.

Experience can be said to be a bundle of knowledge you have acquired over time as a result of application, practising and engaging yourself in the act. With work experience, you stand a shoulder above those who are novices, as it allows you to make career starts or switches much quicker than people with little or no experience.

It is important to start early to acquire experience in the field you want to transition into. Early preparation is the winning card. While you are still seeking employment in your desired career, consider your options and any opportunity you can get to gain work experience.

If you are currently unemployed, consider volunteering. Volunteering options can be part-time or full-time. Some people may find this hard to do, but volunteering is an investment you are making in the future. Yes, it may be tough financially right now, but then, in a real sense, you are not losing out as ultimately you are acquiring skills and hands-on experience that will pay off in the future. Volunteering does not have to take up that much time, but it does entail sacrificing time that would have been spent elsewhere.

Recently, I was in a furniture shop and the business owner told me about a banker who was currently working there every Saturday as a volunteer. The banker was apparently interested in interior décor and was using her spare time to build up her experience in that area. What was even more remarkable was her dedication to it, as she had become the top seller on commission only and had recently even brought in one of her directors to the store to buy furniture for a new office they were furnishing. I have no doubt that when the time comes to finally move on to her dream job, she will have earnt a very good reference from the business owner.

As a matter of fact, I know of many employees who are doing very well working in the place of their dreams today, who started out as volunteers working for free just to learn and add experience on their CVs. Sometimes, we must learn and be patient to pay the price for our own advancement in life. Volunteering is a strategic and easy way to get your foot in the employer's door during a career change. It comes at little or no cost to the employer and I have seen a number of volunteer positions be converted to full-time job offers.

If you are currently employed or if volunteering is not a preferred option, there are other methods you can employ to gain work experience. One of these is taking on additional responsibilities that are similar to that of your desired career. I know a few people in sales and customer service who were able to demonstrate the generalist HR knowledge required for a career transition into human resources. In one particular instance, the candidate was able to demonstrate competencies in recruitment, performance management and training. All the experiences she cited were gained from working as a call centre supervisor, where she was responsible for managing a team of five staff. She was interested in a career in human resources and had begun researching, reading and practising what she had learnt on the team she was assigned to lead. That gave her a decent amount of experience in people management and leadership. She also spoke to the HR manager and other HR professionals regularly on any issues with regards to honing her HR skills. All this was in deliberate preparation for a career change, and it worked for her; at the time of writing this book, she has been in a human resources career for over four years.

Another, often overlooked, option for gaining work experience, is working for oneself. Working for yourself or starting a business is a great way of gaining experience in a new field. This may not be possible for all careers, but it is indeed possible for quite a number of careers. I have met several sales professionals who did some selling on their own, prior to getting the job they wanted. I also know a few recruitment consultants who started off as freelance recruitment consultants before launching into full-blown human resources consultancy. Other examples are of many self-taught computer engineers and programmers. The experience gathered may not be perfect but it is better than none at all. It is a form of preparation, so that when the dream career opportunity comes, you are not found wanting.

When I decided to switch from my role as a Design Engineer to Training Consultant, I took some time off to prepare. This time, I actually saved up and quit my job. I knew that consulting involved a lot of writing and presentations, so I began by buying two books on presentation and training skills. I do like my hard-copy books, and I still have them today. I also conducted a lot of research on the internet. I started practising designing training programmes and using PowerPoint to design training slides. In addition to reading up on training consulting, brushing up on PowerPoint and getting myself abreast in the field of training consulting, I borrowed a projector from my brother. With the projector, I started practising presentation skills. I remember taking the projector to a friend's house once, setting it up over there, presenting before them and asking for their feedback. I was doing all this and, yet, I had no interview in sight. Now, guess what happened as soon as I got an interview at a management consulting firm? I was prepared and I was grateful for all the activities that I had carried out that had brought me to that point.

Just like I shared with you in the chapter Retrain, your career success rests mainly on you and not your boss, your family or even the business that you work for. Don't wait for your employer to figure out how or what your career journey should be. You are in control of your career destiny. It is your life, so take charge!

Going out of your way to gather experience in the field you desire usually means that you go out of your comfort zone. There are instances where people quit their comfortable jobs to either take time off or take up a low-paying job that they consider more aligned with their career goals and fulfilment. While I agree that this can be a tough decision, let's not forget that one of the objectives of gaining experience is to close any existing skills gaps you may have and, ultimately, prepare for the greater reward or a more fulfilling career.

Try answering the questions in the following task. The answers you provide will help you identify what options you have and what actions you can take to gain work experience in your desired field.

Task 4

1. What options do you have to gain work experience in your desired field?

2. What is your preferred option for gaining work experience?

3. What will you commit to doing in the next three, six and twelve months?

5

Consider Internal Vacancies

Sometimes, the career change you need may not necessarily require you switching fields completely, but simply changing job roles within the same organisation. If you already have a job, consider an internal job change rather than looking outward. Let's say you are currently in marketing, but you have always desired a career in finance; rather than looking for that vacancy outside your firm, you can start by exploring the possibilities of being transferred to the department or team within your firm that is more aligned to your career aspirations.

To achieve this, it would require that you speak to one or several people, which may include your manager, someone in human resources, the manager of the desired team, the CEO or anyone else who may be in a position to help you realise your goal.

Internal career changes are not necessarily easy, as you would typically need to make a case as to why you should be considered for the role. For this reason, it is important that you are able to demonstrate what you have done so far to qualify for the role – for example, participated in a training programme, conducted extensive research about the field, undertaken volunteer work, or pursued further studies. You must be able to demonstrate value in the new role. Remember that, beyond your personal ambition, the organisation must also realise benefits and be convinced that transferring you to the new role would not be detrimental to the organisation's bottom-line and growth.

I often hear people say they are passionate about a new career path, but once questioned about what they have done to demonstrate this so-called 'passion', they become mute or begin to reel out one excuse after another. They have no evidence to demonstrate any sense of passion other than a few empty words. That is not real passion. Real passion is full of energy and activity; it propels you to be responsible and do the work. It pushes you to take action and take the steps required to realise your goals. So, when people say they are passionate about a desired career path, I want to know what price they have paid towards achieving it.

A few years ago, I met a lady with twelve years of career experience in customer service and she had a strong desire to start a career in human resources. She attended one of our training programmes on the advice of her HR manager. After attending a few other short courses, she did not have to wait too long before an opening in employee relations within her organisation's HR department came up. Because she had demonstrated her commitment and readiness for the role earlier, she was offered the job. She got the job not just because she had the passion for it, but because she had demonstrated her passion by preparing herself. She had made the necessary investments in the form of money, time and efforts to achieve her goal within the same organisation. Sometimes, the opportunities we seek to move to the next level in our career may be so close to us, within our current place of employment even, that we fail to take advantage of them. Remember, it is often said that 'there is no such thing as luck, it is opportunity meets preparation'.

How well have you prepared for your own career growth? If the opportunity should show up right now, will you be ready to clinch it or would you be found wanting? Maybe you have your eyes focused outside of your organisation, while opportunities for you to achieve the same goal keep passing you by within your current organisation?

When I joined the management consulting firm, I was placed in the strategy team; my transferable analytical and problem-solving skills from the technology field were seen as useful to the team I joined, so that was my first port of call in the consulting field. However, I had always been intrigued by people and human behaviour, and so, after a year, I knew I wanted to focus more on people-related consulting. At the time, I did not know what human resources consulting was all about as it was a somewhat newer field as compared to the traditional, more established fields. I started researching courses in psychology and found one online. It was a diploma course – an intensive four-week programme – held by Middlesex University during the summer as part of their summer school programme. I enrolled for the course, which took up the entire four weeks of my vacation time. Of course, it was a stressful period, as it was supposed to be a vacation, but there I was, waking up earlier than usual and embarking on an intensive programme that included two major assessments. By the time I resumed my job, I was more tired than when I had left.

However, on one faithful day, my CEO saw me and asked me how my vacation had been. I went on to tell him about the Diploma in Psychology I had just gained. He seemed very excited to hear about it and asked that I meet with him in his office to speak about it further. When we met, he went on to explain to me that a new team was being formed and that he had been racking his brain as to which four people to put on the new team. The team would focus on using behavioural psychology tools to improve individual, team and organisational performance. Need I say more?

Today, it sounds like a coincidence, but remember what I said about 'opportunity meets preparation'? It is better to be prepared when the opportunity comes knocking and also be available and let people know what you are doing. By completing the Diploma in Psychology, I had demonstrated my desire to change; the investment was huge for a young professional, as it was self-funded and involved a sizeable amount of time and money that some people are unable to commit to. However, in all of this, I was able to switch careers by staying within the same organisation. Notwithstanding, the key factor that made the transition easy was prior preparation just before an opportunity presented itself.

The other great benefit of internal career changes is that they will not usually pose any threat to your current financial status. You are unlikely to be downgraded or asked to take a pay cut. You are also more familiar with the business and its workings so the transition to a new role is much easier for you.

Despite the advantages of internal vacancies, an internal vacancy in your desired field may not exist in your current job. If this is your situation, feel free to move to the next chapter. However, if your desired role exists in your current organisation, perhaps the answers you provide in the following task can help you secure an internal vacancy before you begin exerting your efforts externally.

Task 5

1. Who can you speak to about your desired career change? Think about people who have the power to positively influence your move.

2. Can you currently demonstrate that you are a good candidate for the new role? Give reason/s for yes or no.

3. How do you intend to qualify for an internal opportunity? What can you do to convince key decision-makers that you are a good fit for the role?

6

Consider the Industry

In the last chapter, we explored the option of making a career change within the same organisation. In this chapter, we will consider the option of making a career change within the same industry.

A career change opportunity may not exist within your organisation, but the opportunity you are seeking could exist within another firm in your industry. A larger firm across the street from your office could be looking for someone with your industry knowledge and skills. A smaller firm could be looking for someone like you to fill a more senior role. Another firm in a highly specialised industry could simply rate industry and business knowledge as the most important competency requirements for the job. These three examples cited are the reality and not the exception when it comes to making a career change.

Let us imagine that you are a sales executive in a bank and desire a career as a financial advisor. There may not be a vacancy in your bank, but your banking experience is an added advantage in the financial services industry. Your banking experience will serve as a great foundation for a financial advisor role within the financial services industry, which cuts across insurance, banks, investment houses and, these days, FinTech, which integrates the financial services and technology industries. Financial advisors work closely with individuals and businesses, developing and offering solutions that can help them meet their financial goals and objectives. For a sales executive, the ability to demonstrate leverage from your existing industry knowledge is strategic to your making a smooth transition to a new career as a financial advisor. Sure, industry knowledge alone may not be considered enough, and that is why we have other chapters focusing on retraining, networking and other things you can do. However, industry knowledge will gain you the leverage that is the key to having one more advantage over another candidate being considered for the same role.

Another reason why industry knowledge gives leverage is that it is closely linked to developing transferable skills. The transferable skills developed can be used in a variety of careers within the industry and even careers outside the industry that have similar characteristics. The characteristics of certain industries often make individuals in those industries develop certain competencies prevalent to that industry. For example, the technology industry is often seen as fast-paced and constantly evolving. It is no surprise that people who work within the technology industry develop competencies that help them adapt to an ever-changing environment. Constantly working in a project-driven environment may make you more comfortable with working to tight deadlines, working to client specifications and being flexible and adaptable. There are other industries and business firms – for example, retail, start-ups and a lot of service-based organisations such as consulting – which require people with similar competencies to those in technology firms.

In highly specialised industries where the systems and processes are unique and maybe even complex, someone with experience in the industry will prove very valuable to firms in that industry. I know a number of engineers who have previously worked in the manufacturing sector but now enjoy varied careers in human resources and sales. Most of them cite that knowledge of the industry was key to their career change. Another example is Paul, who spent most of his career in human resources and is currently a sales director in an oil and gas firm. He had spent a number of years working closely with the sales teams and spent a lot of time working alongside business managers, crafting their sales strategies. The opportunity to move into sales did not happen within his organisation, but, when an opportunity arose in the industry, he gave it a shot and is now enjoying a different career. Yes, experience matters, but in those organisations that are more process-driven, the key ingredient may be interpersonal skills and not so much technical skills. When you leverage opportunities within your industry or sector, you may not have the job role experience, but your knowledge of a certain industry will surely count in your favour.

So, what if you do not want another job but want to start a business instead? The same principle applies. Imagine the leverage you will have because of your knowledge of an industry. Perhaps you have worked in the marketing communications industry and want to start your own communications agency, or you have spent several years in the educational sector and want to start your own school. The first real business I ever started was a training and consulting firm. The experience that I gained in the consulting industry definitely provided the leverage to consider such a business area. Sure, we do not need to work in or even understand an industry to manage a business in that area, but, when we do, it can only be to our advantage, which is a big plus for us as we can save on the costs that come with learning a new business.

When making a career change, the key consideration is to look for any similarities between where you are coming from and where you want to go. It is easier to start on familiar ground than a place of uncertainty and little knowledge.

There are two more things you should consider when trying to make a career change within an industry. The first suggestion is to stay informed of the opportunities in the industry. Spend time reading up on news, changes in policies or new developments. Some industries have special networking forums and associations; you can also join these to ensure that you have a valuable network that you can always leverage. Without being well-informed, there is a high chance that you will miss out on career opportunities within the industry.

The second suggestion is to be open-minded. By this, I mean do not limit your career search to just one job role, as an opportunity for a career change can open up in something that appears different but may really be a step in the right direction. Sometimes, a career change journey is a direct move from one type of role to the desired role, but, sometimes, it is an indirect move that involves taking transit roles that are not exactly the desired role but are a step closer to it. Sometimes, if a field is difficult to get into, the key is to examine the key competence required for your desired role and look for opportunities where you can gain that competence. All jobs require a set of competencies and getting the right mix of competencies, including industry exposure, can improve your chances of landing in your dream career.

Today, as many industries are overlapping and converging, it takes a degree of open-mindedness to see opportunities in similar roles and similar industries and take advantage of them.

Try answering the questions in the following task to help you discover whether there are opportunities around you that you can take advantage of.

Task 6

1. Can you identify some companies in your industry that you should consider? If yes, identify them and write them down; if no, then consider conducting some research to identify the companies in your industry. Remember to include overlapping industries.

2. What transferable skills have you gained from your industry?

3. What specialised knowledge and skills have you gained from your industry?

4. Where else can the knowledge and skills you have gained from your industry be valuable?

7

Consider Easier Entry Points

All careers have easier entry points. By this, I mean those roles that have a lower barrier to entry. They are usually jobs that do not require a high degree of technical skill. They can also be jobs that serve as an apprentice or assistant role to a more specialised career. A lot of these roles require less formal training than your typical professional career.

For example, in the field of human resources, an area with a lower-barrier entry point is recruitment. A lot of HR professionals start off in recruitment and then later transition into other more specialised aspects. Even entry-level staff in HR are often given routine recruitment tasks such as shortlisting and scheduling applicants for interviews. Examples from the legal profession are paralegals and court clerks. In the medical field, you have dental assistants who help dentists in dental clinics, and in the accounting profession you have accounting technicians or clerks who assist qualified or more senior accountants.

An entry point allows you to get your foot in the door while gaining valuable experience that you can use to build upon and grow into your dream role. A good way of finding out which careers have easier entry points is by asking those in your desired role which jobs have a lower entry threshold; then consider taking that route if your preferred role is not forthcoming. Doing this doesn't mean you are giving up on your primary goal; it just means you are taking a more flexible approach that will eventually lead you to your desired goal.

Internships and apprenticeships can also be seen as taking an easier entry point, as they both entail starting off as someone who is learning the ropes from a more experienced person. This strategy also works when starting a new business. You can choose to start off by understudying a business before starting up a similar business.

Felix started off as a cleaner before launching his own cleaning business. Cleaning jobs are very easy to get as they are minimum-wage jobs in many countries. Even if you do not want to get a cleaning job, it is very easy to get cleaning experience; just start by cleaning in your own home. Another option may be to start a simplified form of what could become a complex business, such as starting with a home-based bakery in your kitchen instead of opening a full-blown custom-built industrialised bakery straight away. The important thing about all this is to still keep the dream big, but start small.

Unfortunately, one of the reasons why many people don't adopt this approach is because of personal pride and financial commitments. Some look down on lower-level roles and others cannot afford to, or do not want to, make financial sacrifices. They stay tied to one place while gnashing their teeth about how badly they want change. While I am not completely faulting personal circumstances and choices, I must also add that, in life, sometimes you have to stoop to conquer; you go low before going high. I have seen employees deliberately choose to take up lower- or entry-level roles for career paths they desire, rather than stay put in high-paying jobs that they have no passion for.

Taking lower-level positions is the price that some people pay just to see that they achieve their career ambition. The question is: Would you be willing to do that if that is the option before you? Remember, it is a means to an end and not an end in itself. There are different ways to get to the same destination; hence, your entry point is simply your unique route to your final destination. From my experience in life, I can surely say that it is not how you start that matters the most, but how you finish. The most important thing is the end goal, not the process or the journey, but the final destination. So, that entry-level role you may be disregarding may just be the key to unlocking the door to that great career ambition you have.

The following questions will help you examine any opportunities that may present low barriers to entry into your desired career path.

Task 7

1. What existing jobs or roles can serve as a stepping stone to your desired career?

2. From what sources can you seek information about careers related to your dream role? Consider people and resources, such as books and the internet.

3. How can you use the answers given in questions 1 and 2 to move a step closer to your dream career?

8

Get Better at Networking

While trying to change careers, one of the resources you must learn to tap into is your current network and that of others. The role of networking with the right people in creating opportunities for career advancement cannot be overemphasised in today's world. The world is getting increasingly connected, so you cannot afford to keep yourself isolated. The concept of 'six degrees of separation' is the idea that every human is no more than six people away from each other. In the realm of social media, that number is said to shrink by half. Whether that is true or not, the key lesson here is that having quality relationships with the right people opens up new possibilities and opportunities for success in your career path.

As long as people continue to carry out activities, our lives will always be impacted by those we know. Therefore, one of the habits you must develop is to cultivate quality relationships with people in and outside of your workplace. Know people and let them know you.

Even though your success in your career depends on a lot of your effort, people still have a role to play in creating the needed leverage or opening the doors that you need to step through for your next career. People with good people skills are more likely to succeed in their careers when compared to those who have poor interpersonal skills. If you have a quality network of people that you have nurtured over time, it is much easier for them to extend their support to you in your desire to change careers.

Let people in your network know about your desire to change your career. The more people know, the more soldiers you have helping you conquer your battle. All you usually need is just one person – the right person or the right connection – but it is not always obvious who this person is, so we have to spread our net far and wide like true fishermen.

Prior to changing careers from telecoms to management consulting, I kept telling everyone who would listen that I wanted to pursue a career in training consulting. In three separate conversations, everyone I told kept telling me to try a particular firm – well, guess what? I eventually met someone who did not just end up telling me to try contacting the same consulting firm, but asked me to send him my CV because he had access to the hiring partner of the firm. I forwarded my CV to him the following morning and was called for an interview in record time.

However, this did not happen in my backyard; I was out and about. The ultimate connection that helped me with that opportunity was my friend's boss. I went to my friend's office after work and got introduced to his boss who asked me what I was doing at the time. I explained to him that I was transitioning from a previous career to training consultancy. I went out to meet people. I was showcasing myself and was not stuck behind a computer sending CVs and applications online. Online networking is great, but offline and face-to-face communication is more effective.

A simple phone call from someone within your network may just be all that you need to get you a job in your desired career field. Get to know people, take time to connect with the right people and build emotional bank deposits with them.

Do not be that person who is locked in the cubicle of their own world, never taking time out to build relationships in and out of their work environment. Be accessible. Be visible. Ensure that you can be found and be approachable. Develop your interpersonal skills. Become someone that others can effectively relate to. Be that person who adds value to and connects with others. People tend to assist people who communicate and relate well with them. Always remember that great things happen through people – people at all levels and with different responsibilities. So never underestimate the power of effective networking and how it can assist you in your career goals and pursuits.

I, for one, get so many job-related requests, and when opportunities like those come, I only ever remember the people within my network and who are regularly in touch with me. If you are the individual that hardly connects or stays in touch, it would be unlikely that the opportunities that arise would be extended your way. If you find it a little difficult to network with others, then you may want to try more discreet methods initially as you gradually build the confidence to develop the skill. Online methods such as sending messages, emails and joining online forums are also forms of networking. You can build quality networks online; the key factor is building a relationship that is meaningful.

You can also start attending professional events within and outside your sector. Be more interested in others. Make it a habit to use your gifts to help others. Extend a hand of support to your team members, your current employer and those outside your field. Create a profile on LinkedIn and on other social media platforms. Join professional organisations. Sign up for online and offline forums that allow you to meet the right people. Go out of your way to know recruiters. Keep in touch with past colleagues and employers. Invest in quality books and audio and video programmes that teach you how to network effectively and build people skills. Get more involved in your community.

One of the things you may also need to audit is your current network, ensuring that you are not exposing yourself to toxic, career-limiting relationships that don't bring out the best in you. It is possible that the current crop of people around you is undermining your self-esteem, causing you to lose confidence in yourself and preventing you from developing better people skills or ambition. If that is true, then that is also an area that needs some work. Networking doesn't mean you should allow the wrong people into your space. Make a deliberate effort to relate with people who bring out the best in you, who add value to your dreams and who help you develop and grow as a person.

I must add that the art of networking is a tricky one, and, in as much as people try to be strategic about whom they network with, there is an element of luck involved in it, just as in most things in life. Referrals and opportunities do not always come from the most obvious places. Personally, I have enjoyed value-adding relationships from all levels and types of people. I have received work-based referrals from lower-level staff and been informed of a business opportunity by an office cleaner. One example I will always remember was a business referral from an unemployed young lady I was mentoring at the time. There was a business opportunity for a training consultancy, and I was the first person she called and asked to contact the new Head of Human Resources. Imagine my surprise, then, if I had thought she was too low down to offer me an opportunity. I work with HR directors and managing directors all the time, but I must say that I get more referrals from staff lower down the ladder.

My point really is about building relationships. Relationships make the world go round. The more quality relationships you have, the better the support network you will have and the closer you will be to any desired career. Trust the power of networks – someone in your network will know someone who knows someone else who you need to make that career change a reality. Get out there. Now!

The following task is designed to help you assess the current state of your network and devise an action plan to improve it.

Task 8

1. Consider the following channels of your network: family, friends, community, school/work colleague and online.

2. On a scale of 1 to 10, how do you rate the relationships you have within each channel of your network?

3. What can you do to improve your rating in each area?

9

Plan Your Finances

Most career changes are geared towards having more fulfilling careers. Without a doubt, a lot of career changes aim for an ultimate advancement in financial status.

Some people are able to change careers without any impact on their present financial status, while other career changes require you to make financial investments as a step towards achieving your dream career. This may be necessary to either retrain or gain experience in a new field. A loss in earnings is a very crucial consideration during a career change, and it should be said that some career changers are not able to persist in their career pursuits due to financial obligations or poor financial habits.

Planning your finances is a critical factor that must be taken seriously as you prepare to make a career change. Financial decisions and their impact are important because, as much as they affect you as an individual, their impact often extends to dependants and loved ones. For instance, a career change can affect a couple's finances at home. In fact, finances have been said to be the number one cause of relationship issues that end in divorce. A solid financial plan can help you handle the initial pressure and anxiety that come with a career transition.

There are two main financial planning considerations to think about when making a career change. The first is to save your finances and the second is to manage your spending habits.

A rule of thumb in saving for a career change is to save at least the equivalent of six months' salary. However, if you will be undergoing some form of training for an extended period, you may need to have much more saved up to ensure that you have enough funds to manage the entire duration of your transition. If your career change results in a pay cut or requires you to stop earning an income in order to receive training, you will need to carefully consider how you intend to meet your financial obligations during the transition. Saving is much harder if you are already on a low income or no income; whatever the case, you still need to plan to cover your financial obligations. If you are earning a lower income, you will need to save for a longer period – long enough to ensure that your savings can cover any period of loss in earnings.

When Angela wanted to change careers from sales to technology, she already had over ten years' experience selling technology solutions to companies in the United States. However, she wanted a role that would involve working directly with clients to assist them in developing solutions. She also felt that she needed a change of environment; so, she opted for a Master's degree in the United Kingdom. Decisions such as this are obviously cost-intensive. In her case, the Master's programme was 24 months long, so she had to save enough to cover her finances for the next two years. Some of the additional expenses she had to consider included mortgage costs, for which you would need to plan for the worst-case scenario, even with a tenant renting your apartment (so plan for a situation such as the tenant moving out unexpectedly, which happened in Angela's case). Angela had to ensure that she had saved enough to sustain her two years' loss in earnings and the additional expenses that came with studying in another country.

Bear in mind that when your career change involves having to retrain, you must plan the entire cost of the programme. In some cases, this not only includes the cost of the training programme, but also other things such as transport, accommodation and living expenses. Not everyone can afford these types of costs, but all forms of training will involve some type of cost. Short courses often allow you to maintain your current job while retraining, but they still eat into your time. Time is a major resource, as all the time spent doing one thing has the opportunity cost of forgoing something else of a similar value.

Aside from my initial career change through a Master's degree straight out of university, I have managed to keep subsequent career change-related training to short courses. With the advent of e-learning and online courses, it is much easier now to learn without making the huge commitments required of classroom-based training.

Changing careers is a life-changing experience that requires a thoughtful approach. It can affect your lifestyle and reshuffle your existing priorities. It involves a change in the status quo, and change is often fraught with emotional responses. In some cases, you may be required to change location within the same country or move to a different country, and if the process is not well-planned and managed, it can affect your life negatively.

Planning your finances prepares you for the days ahead and helps you allocate financial resources in the best way possible. It gives you clarity not only on how to spend your money but also guides you on how to multiply it or at least make it last longer. Some people quit high-paying jobs and begin to experience financial stress after only a few months. This may happen not because they didn't have enough money saved up, but due to poor financial habits that they carried over. Some people get so used to spending money in a certain way that they fail to unlearn their old money culture even when they have less income available. Certain habits are a sure way to dwindle your savings fast. Two money-dwindling acts that easily come to mind are eating out and taking vacations. There are, of course, many other forms of mindless spending, especially in these days of impulsive internet buying where one click is all you need to make a very expensive purchase.

If you are expecting an impending pay cut, it is wise for you to review your spending behaviour by cutting down on impulse purchases and redirecting your spending to more essential items. By planning your finances, you don't just learn better money management skills, but you also know whether or not you need to create alternative sources of income to support your lifestyle and take care of any shortfall.

If you are planning to start a business, the need for better financial planning is increased as the financial risks and exposure are much more. You may need to apply for a loan or borrow from friends and family to raise initial capital. The start of any business involves more spending than generating income, so you really need a good buffer, as well as a positive financial track record should you need to borrow.

Ultimately, financial planning boils down to personal commitment and self-discipline. Always be reminded that your financial success in life does not depend on how much you earn, but on how much you are able to manage your finances. One of the reasons why some people hesitate or give excuses for not making the needed career change is because they are unprepared to deal with their financial inadequacies. If you are stuck in this same reality, then now is the time to start schooling yourself on issues concerning personal finance management. Make a decision to be disciplined with the way you handle your finances rather than giving 1,001 reason why you cannot achieve your desired career goal.

For most, the decision to change careers is a bold one where you, at some point, bite the bullet and stop procrastinating. Whatever your unique situation, ensure that you plan your finances in good time. Do not assume that things will figure themselves out along the way, as they usually don't, and, by the time you realise it, you will already be struggling.

The questions in the upcoming task will help you explore the possible impact of a planned career change on your finances. By considering the possible impact, it becomes so much easier to develop a plan to mitigate the impending financial risks.

Task 9

1. How will a career change impact your current finances?

2. What options are available to enable you to manage your finances in preparation for any foreseen financial impact? Consider any saving requirements and adjustments required to spending habits.

3. What preferred actions can you take to mitigate the financial impact of the career change?

10

Set Goals and Execute

Like everything else we desire in life, we have to set goals and decide, at some point, when we should have achieved certain tasks. Never leave things to chance. Set relevant goals and key milestones for what you want to achieve. Be deliberate in planning the next level of advancement in your career.

Most of us are familiar with the adage 'if you fail to plan, you plan to fail'. Some of us have heard it so many times that it fails to ring a bell in our minds anymore. However, the words remain true. Goals are often achieved when they begin with a plan – a concerted effort to achieve a goal.

Since visions can be far-fetched and more long-term, what we often need for a short- to medium-term career change are goals. An example could be a goal to transition to a new career in project management in the next twelve to eighteen months.

Goals must be SMART: they must be Specific, Measurable, Achievable, Realistic and Time-bound. If you cannot measure a goal, you will struggle to manage it. Set smaller, but more manageable, goals that you can achieve along the way. Smaller goals are called milestones and do not appear daunting. They serve as a feedback mechanism and help you check your progress. They also ensure that you do not wait until it is too late to realise that you have fallen off the course of your plan.

Setting timelines is crucial to setting goals, as they activate a sense of urgency as well as keep us accountable. Without timelines, we are bound by nothing, and so our goals do not have an expected date of realisation. Without timelines, we may never achieve our dreams in our lifetime. Giving ourselves timelines gives us something to look forward to and puts things into perspective. It helps us plan our lives by paying attention to areas that require intricate plans, such as our finances, work schedules and families.

Sometimes, we may need to go as far as giving ourselves ultimatums. Sure, there will always be unforeseen circumstances, but we can deal with them when they arise. Procrastination, they say, is the thief of time, and time is the real currency on this earth. Every day we spend doing something not aligned to our goals is an opportunity lost and which can never be recovered. So, let us embrace deadlines and stay motivated. Running away from deadlines is only postponing your goals, limiting your growth and extending your misery.

Our goals need to be achievable and not easy; they must be inspiring and not demotivating. Goals must stretch us, and stretching us often makes us feel uncomfortable, but, then, such stretching is what develops us ultimately. Specify what steps you are going to take in order to make a successful career transition. Then ask yourself what you will do, starting right now, to make it happen and in what sequence.

Beyond developing beautiful plans and setting goals must be actions; actions turn plans into reality. Too many people create desires and plans, but never take action. When you have listed the steps you need to take to achieve your career change, take action as quickly as possible. Talking about plans and writing them down are non-value adding activities if they are not followed by actions. You cannot realise a plan if you don't follow through on it. Somebody has to work the plan and that person is you.

Planning is noble, but all the plans in the world amount to nothing without execution. Execution is the art of getting things done.

Execute!

I have met people who whine about their current job and how they need a change. But when asked what they are doing to make that change happen, they cannot tell you about anything tangible. They keep themselves stuck in the same spot, year in and year out, without initiating a move. They have no restraint in telling you all the reasons why they have not made a move. They make themselves feel better by relaying a long list of excuses. The sad thing about this is that time waits for no one. Often, with age comes more obligations. The perfect moment does not exist. If you are already in a miserable situation, why extend your misery? It will not happen overnight, but you can start taking baby steps today. Doing something or anything is better than doing nothing. Doing nothing has a definite destination, and that place is called 'nowhere'.

Be willing to pay the price of your own success. If your career change requires that you enrol for a special course or acquire a new skill, plan to do it and go out of your way to do it. If it requires that you need to build up your interpersonal relationships with people – which often it does – then don't hesitate, get started today. Success often comes with discomfort and doing what we would not ordinarily do. There is a reason behind the term 'growing pains'; most growth comes with some form of discomfort or pain. Stepping out of the comfort zone is not something that comes naturally to most, but we must get uncomfortable to get comfortable. Set your goals, align your priorities and go for them. Write down your career change plans based on your preferred course of action and be ready to get to work.

Just do it!

One thing that all success stories have in common is that they all involve taking action. Sometimes, what you need to do to achieve your career change may be long-term, yet there are still small blocks of actions you need to start laying today to be able to take that big step tomorrow. Don't wait for all your ducks to line up before you get started on the journey. A journey of a thousand miles, they say, begins with one single step. So, if you are thinking of changing careers soon or in the future, I can bet you there are little steps you can start taking today and every day to better position yourself for a successful move.

Try answering the following questions to help you explore your career goals and devise actionable plans to steer you in the right direction.

Task 10

1. What is your current career goal? Where do you want to be within the next eighteen months?

2. What is your current reality? Have you done anything so far to get you closer to your career goal?

3. What goals can you set now to achieve your current career goal? Remember, goals must be SMART (Specific, Measurable, Achievable, Realistic and Time-bound).

4. What specific action will you take now and within the next eighteen months?

11

Bonus Tip: Be Patient

Sometimes, great things take time to happen. Even after all is said and done, all your plans and preparations have been put in place, a career change can be a waiting game that involves waiting for the opportunity to finally sail your ship in the right direction.

For some people, a career change happens quickly, but for most a career change is a deliberate effort that requires careful planning, resilience and patience. Do not expect success to happen overnight; this only happens to a rare minority. Set a realistic timeline for your career change and be sure to stay hopeful and diligent. If it happens earlier, great news; but if it does not, remain positive, for it is only a matter of time.

Never ever give up on yourself, and, remember, it is never too late to keep working towards your dreams. A career change can happen at any time and stage in life; it can happen at 19 and it can happen at 60. John Pemberton invented Coca-Cola at 55, while Harland Sanders began Kentucky Fried Chicken (KFC) at 62. Sadly, you have no excuse.

If you have tried to make a career change and it didn't work out as planned, don't throw in the towel or develop a negative attitude. While it is important that you shouldn't lose faith in your desired career, it is equally important that you don't stop adding tremendous value to your current situation. Successful people do not allow setbacks or failure to stop them. If your application was rejected, try again.

Have a big vision for your career, refuse to resign yourself to mediocrity, but have the patience to work the process. Sometimes, patience means you giving yourself more time to further develop the capacity, relationships and credibility in your current situation before moving to the next. Don't be in such a hurry that you fail to prepare yourself and plan out your transition; instead, spend your time better preparing yourself for your new career.

While you are being patient, remember to also stay informed about what is happening in the industry of your desired career. If you are employed, get yourself involved in the best practices and be willing to learn things beyond your job function. Develop strategic relationships in and outside your organisation and invest in your personal growth.

Bonus Tip: Be Patient

If you still find yourself feeling discouraged by things not working out the way you want, maybe you might want to start investing in activities that help you develop the right positive mental attitude. These days, it is not uncommon to find people investing in hiring a coach to help them achieve goals in important areas of their lives, such as their careers. A career coach's goal is to help you achieve your career goals much quicker than if you were pursuing them on your own.

Let nothing stop you from believing the best for yourself. Remember, you are never too old to achieve greatness. Keep working the process until it works.

The next set of questions are designed to help you focus on any other actions or attitudes that can get you closer to your career goals.

Now get going and good luck – your next career awaits you with open arms!

Task 11

1. How else can you prepare yourself before your desired career role is achieved?

2. What specific actions will you take?

3. How will you ensure that you maintain a positive mental attitude?

About the Author

Adora Ikwuemesi is a speaker, writer and globally certified professional in the field of human resources management. She is a trained coach with a Bachelor's degree in Economics from the University of Reading and a Master's degree in Information Technology from Cranfield University, both in the United Kingdom.

With a career spanning the fields of technology, telecoms, management consulting, human resources management and entrepreneurship, Adora has first-hand experience of the challenges faced in making a career change. By using the practical approach revealed in her book, she successfully changed her career five times.

Adora is the founder of Kendor Consulting, a human resources management consultancy firm specialising in learning and development solutions. She is also the founder and host of the annual Human Resources Boot Camp Conference, a platform she established to explore new paradigms for reinventing people management practices.

Adora continues to host and speak at events that focus on developing people to realise their full potential. Through numerous articles, training workshops and conferences, she has helped thousands of people make progress in the achievement of their career goals.

Find out more about Adora at **www.adoraikwuemesi.com**

Printed in Great Britain
by Amazon